IDIOMS FOR IELTS SPEAKING

Master 500+ Idioms In Use Explained In 10 Minutes A Day

RACHEL MITCHELL

ISBN: 9781717943781

Text copyright © 2018 [Rachel Mitchell]

TABLE OF CONTENT

INTRODUCTION...5

LETTER A..6

LETTER B..9

LETTER C..13

LETTER D 16

LETTER E..19

LETTER F..20

LETTER G...24

LETTER H...29

LETTER I...32

LETTER K...36

LETTER L..37

LETTER M...40

LETTER N 43

LETTER O 44

LETTER P 47

LETTER R..50

LETTER S 52

LETTER T..55

LETTER U...57

LETTER W 58

CONCLUSION 59

CHECK OUT OTHER BOOKS...60

INTRODUCTION

Thank you and congratulate you for downloading the book *"Idioms for IELTS Speaking: Master 500+ Idioms In Use Explained In 10 Minutes A Day"*

This book is well designed and written by an experienced native teacher from the USA who has been teaching IELTS for over 10 years. She really is the expert in training IELTS for students at each level. In this book, she will provide you with *over 500 essential Idioms For IELTS Speaking* **explained** with examples to help you **speak English more natural and confidently** and easily achieve an **8.0+** for the IELTS speaking *Fluency and Accuracy* and *Lexical Resource Band Score*, even if your vocabulary is not rich enough from the beginning.

As the author of this book, Rachel Mitchell believes that this book will be **an indispensable reference** and **trusted guide** for you who may want to maximize your *Fluency and Accuracy* band score in the IELTS speaking exam. Once you read this book, I guarantee you that you will have learned an extraordinarily wide range of useful, and practical IELTS Idioms that will help you **talk like a native speaker**, become **a successful IELTS taker** as well as you will even become **a successful English user** in work and in life **within a short period of time** only.

Take action today and start getting **8.0 + in IELTS speaking** TOMORROW!

Thank you again for purchasing this book, and I hope you enjoy it.

LETTER A

At all costs = at any costs: *to do everything you can to achieve something regardless of the difficulty, and expense involved.*

His dream is to become a great lawyer at all costs.

They were determined to win the game at any cost.

As easy as pie: *very easy.*

The test is as easy as pie.

Searching for beautiful flower images online is as easy as pie nowadays.

After so many years as an English teacher, doing taxes is as easy as pie for me.

A drop in the ocean: *a very small amount compared to what is required or needed.*

The amount of money that he gave me last night is just a drop in the ocean compared to what I needed.

I feel what I am doing is just a drop in the ocean.

Actions speak louder than words: *used for expressing that what you do something is more important than just talking about it.*

He usually talks about the importance of charity but never does anything. Actions speak louder than words

Because actions speak louder than words, do not talk much, just act.

A hot potato: *a controversial topic, issue or situation.*

Money policy is fast becoming a hot potato.

The issues of abortion and tax have become real hot potatoes in my country these days.

Against the clock: *to do something quickly to finish it before a particular time.*

She is working against the clock to finish her essay by today.

We have to work against the clock to meet the deadline (to finish the project on time).

A rip-off: *something that is unreasonably expensive.*

We shouldn't have spent so much. That's a rip-off.

$60 for a cup of coffee is a complete rip-off.

At first: *in the beginning.*

Don't judge anyone or anything at first sight.

Try again if you fail at first.

Around the corner: *coming very soon.*

Tom is quite nervous because his exam is just around the corner.

Spring is just around the corner.

A mile a minute: *very quickly.*

He walks a mile a minute and is very difficult to keep up with.

She is talking a mile a minute.

A man of his word: *someone who does what he promises to do.*

He is obviously a man of his word. You can trust him.

Tom is a man of his word. He always does what he says he is going to.

A ladies man: *a man that loves spending time and flirting with women.*

He is known as a ladies man.

Tom has the reputation for being quite a ladies' man.

Ace a test: *to do very well in a test/ to get a very high score on a test.*

You need to study hard to ace a test.

She had actually aced a test in math, a subject that had never come easily for her.

A bad egg: *someone who is bad and untrustworthy.*

That guy is a bad egg. Don't trust him.

Be careful of her. She is a bad egg.

LETTER B

Bump into somebody: *meet somebody by chance.*

I bumped into her at the mall.

I bumped into him at the pub a couple of days ago.

Be out of your depth: *expressing that you are in a situation that is too difficult or dangerous to deal with.*

She is used to teaching English writing but she was out of my depth when she had to teach English listening.

Behind the times: *expressing that something is not modern, old-fashioned, obsolete or out of date.*

If you don't want to fall behind the times, read the newspaper every day.

If you think the world is flat, you are behind the times.

The marketing plan for their products is a little behind the times.

To be up in arms about something: *expressing that you are very angry or upset about something.*

The local residents have been up in arms about the tax increase.

Be sick and tired of something: *to be very frustrated, annoyed, bored with or very unhappy about something.*

He is sick and tired of listening to clients' complaints.

I'm sick and tired of working the same tasks every day.

Bend over backwards: *to do everything you can to help or to please someone.*

Sarah bent over backwards to make her new husband feel at home.

Tom bent over backwards to please his girlfriend.

To be under the weather: *do not feel well; feel sick.*

Tom was feeling a bit under the weather today, so he chose to take the day off.

I'm feeling a bit under the weather. I think I've caught a cold.

Blew me away: *when something blows you away, it impresses you very much or makes you very excited.*

He just totally blew me away with his singing.

It blew me away when I heard that my little brother is going to get married.

That song really blew me away.

Back to the drawing board: *to start doing something again.*

I'll go back to the drawing board if my proposal is not accepted.

Our experiment was a failure, so we need to be back to the drawing board.

Burn the midnight oil: *to stay up late, to work late at night.*

Tom is going to take his exams next week, so he's burning the midnight oil.

Sarah had to burn the midnight oil to complete her essay.

Bare your heart: *to reveal your secret thoughts and feelings to someone.*

She decided to bare her heart through text messages to her closest friends.

Tom is too shy to bare his heart to his girlfriend.

To buy into something: *to accept something.*

Tom's never bought into this idea that his girlfriend has to be thin to be attractive.

Her boss didn't buy into her reason for being late at work.

To be bouncing off the walls: *to be so busy.*

It's like that you're bouncing off the walls.

The workers seem to be bouncing off the walls.

Be bummed out: *to be sad, depressed.*

She was bummed out when she heard bad news that her mom was ill.

Tom didn't get the promotion and he felt really bummed out.

To be dolled up: *to get all dressed up to look attractive.*

Lucy was dolled up in jewels for the party last night.

She spent an hour getting dolled up for the celebration.

To be out of this world: *to be extraordinary or impressive.*

Views from the hotel room are out of the world.

We are in a place that is out of the world.

To be dressed to kill: *to be dressed beautifully (wearing very smart or fashionable clothes)*

His wife was dressed to kill at the party last night.

Lucy is always dressed to kill on every Saturday night.

To break the news: *to disclose important information to someone.*

I don't want to break the news to him.

I think that we should not break the news at the moment.

You should try to break the news to her gently.

(To) butt in: *to interrupt; to interfere a conversation or activity without being invited.*

Stop butting in on my personal life!

Tom doesn't want Mary to butt in his personal life.

(To) blow it: *to fail to take advantage of a chance or an opportunity.*

You blew it, Tom!

He blew it. He lost the customer.

Big shot: *an important or powerful person.*

My brother is a big shot in advertising.

Her boyfriend is a big shot in the film industry.

Behind the times: *old-fashioned; out of date.*

His car is a bit behind the times.

If you don't want to fall behind the times, you should read the newspaper every day.

Be an item: *if two people are an item, they are dating and have a romantic relationship.*

Tom and Mary are an item.

Jack and Cindy are an item. They finally made it official.

Blew one's top: *lose one's temper (very angry or irritate).*

Tom's father blew his top when he found out that Tom had damaged his car.

Mary blew her top when she heard that her boyfriend had gone out with another girl.

Bring home the bacon: *to earn money by working to support the family.*

Women are supposed to raise the children and men will bring home the bacon.

Tom and his wife both bring home the bacon.

LETTER C

Cut it out!: *stop it; stop doing that.*

That music is really annoying. Cut it out!

Would you two cut it out and keep quiet? I'm trying to sleep.

Call it a day: *to stop working, to end a job.*

Mike, let's call it a day. It's really late.

Time to call it a day, guys. See you tomorrow!

Chill out: *to relax; to calm down.*

Chill out! We'll get there on time!

Come on! Let's sit down and chill out!

I think you need to chill out a little bit by watching a movie.

Cut corners: *to save money (to do something in the cheapest way).*

The government cut corners and put everyone in danger when they built the school with bad materials.

Remember that we want only the best, no cutting corners on this job.

We have to learn how to cut corners when we have five children to bring up.

Chicken out: *to become too frightened/scared to do something.*

Tom wanted to go skydiving, but he chickened out at the last minute.

She chickened out when she saw how deep the water was.

He was going to do a parachute jump, but he chickened out at the last second.

To cut class = to play hooky = to ditch class: *to deliberately not go to a class when you should be there.*

This is the second time this week Tom has cut class.

If you play hooky again, the teacher will be very angry.

Couch potato: *somebody who is lazy and inactive.*

He is a great couch potato; he can watch TV 24 hours a day.

Since Mary lost her job, she has become a couch potato.

Cold fish: *an unfriendly person.*

Her father is a real cold fish. I've never seen him laugh.

Sarah is a cold fish. She rarely talks to her colleagues.

To catch someone red-handed: *to capture someone in the act.*

He was caught red-handed using drugs.

The thieves were caught red-handed attempting to break into a house.

Count on: *to depend on someone to do what you want.*

She is very busy, don't count on her assistance.

You cannot count on him because he's too irresponsible.

(to) cut it out: *to stop (doing) something.*

I'm trying to sleep, cut it out, please!

The kids were playing games and I told them to cut it out.

Crack of dawn: *(a time) very early in the morning.*

My mom got up at the crack of dawn.

You should go to bed early since we have to leave at the crack of dawn tomorrow.

Crocodile tears: *tears or crying that are not sincere.*

She showed her crocodile tears when her stepmother died.

Don't shed crocodile tears over her death.

Her crocodile tears fool nobody.

Cost an arm and a leg: *to be very expensive.*

The movie is interesting, but the tickets cost an arm and a leg.

The car cost him an arm and a leg.

Catch one's breath: *to rest for a moment after exercise to restore normal breathing.*

He stopped running and tried to catch his breath.

She stopped and placed her hand on his arm to catch her breath.

Come down with: *to become ill with a particular illness.*

She has come down with the flu.

He had come down with a cold.

Can't stand (someone or something): *to hate or dislike someone or something very much.*

She can't stand to hear her parents arguing.

I can't stand traffic jam in rush hour.

LETTER D

Drop someone a line: *to send a note or a short letter to someone.*

I'll drop Peter a line to say thanks for his help.

I promise I will drop you a line as soon as I arrive home safely.

Don't judge a book by its cover: *you shouldn't judge someone or something only from their appearance.*

That woman may look very slow and awkward, but don't judge a book by its cover. She is a very intelligent woman in her circle.

I know I look serious in my picture, hope you don't judge a book by its cover.

Down in the dumps: *feeling very unhappy, depressed, sad.*

Tom has been feeling down in the dumps ever since he lost his job.

Peter seems to be down in the dumps since he broke up with his girlfriend last week.

Day in, day out: *done repeatedly every day over a long period of time.*

Eating the same food day in, day out is very boring.

I really hate doing the same boring tasks day in, day out.

Down to earth: *someone who is practical, realistic and friendly.*

He is a down-to-earth and friendly person.

I like his down-to-earth and hardworking spirit.

Down the road: *in the future.*

It can be achieved down the road.

This deal will be beneficial down the road.

Down in the dumps: *to feel unhappy or really depressed.*

Tom was down in the dumps after he lost his job.

Lucy has been down in the dumps since she failed her driving test.

My sister has been down in the dumps since her dog died.

Down the drain: *to be completely lost, destroyed or wasted.*

All our effort went down the drain.

A lot of money went down the drain by misuse of funds.

Down and out: *have no money, a job, or a shelter.*

Tom was completely down and out after he lost his job.

After her house burned down, Lucy was completely down and out.

Dime a dozen: *very common and not very valuable.*

Teachers like her are a dime a dozen.

His ideas are dime a dozen.

Drive someone crazy: *to make him or her upset or annoyed.*

Tom quit his job because his boss drove him crazy every time he went to work.

The constant noise drove me crazy.

To drive someone nuts: *to make someone very crazy or annoyed.*

The fact that he's over at her house everyday drives her nuts.

He quit his job since his boss drove him nuts every time he went to work.

(to) drive someone crazy: *to make someone upset or annoyed very much.*

It drives Tom crazy that I tell people I am actually younger than he is.

His untidiness drives his mom crazy.

(to) do one's best: *to try your best (to try as hard as possible).*

Although he was tired, he did his best.

She did her best to win the game.

LETTER E

Explore all avenues: *to try everything in order to find a solution and avoid trouble.*

It is a difficult thing to do; therefore, we must explore all avenues if we really want it done.

Every time one turns around: *very often, too often.*

He asks me for some money every time I turn around.

My mom shouts at me every time I turn around.

Eager beaver: *a very hardworking and enthusiastic person.*

My boss is an eager beaver.

Her father is a real eager beaver. He usually works 12 hours a day.

Eyes are bigger than one's stomach: *to take more food than you can possibly eat.*

I'm afraid that your eyes are bigger than your stomach. You can't eat all this.

To eat like a bird: *to eat very little.*

Jane eats like a bird, no wonder she can keep herself so slim.

Don't make too much for lunch because she eats like a bird.

LETTER F

Figure something out: *find a way to solve a problem.*

I think Peter is smart enough to figure out what to do.

I'm surprised when Lucy figured it out quickly.

Fill in for someone: *to temporarily do another person's work or task.*

Mary's colleague filled in for her while she was sick.

The French teacher was sick and Mr. Mike filled in for her.

Find one's feet: *to become confident or comfortable in a new situation.*

It took him a week to find his feet in his job.

It was difficult when I moved to a new city, but I eventually found my feet.

To face up to = to confront: *to accept and deal with a difficult situation in a direct way.*

He faces up to two years in prison and a $50,000 fine.

Finally, the married couple faced up to their money problems.

To fish for a compliment: *to try and get a compliment from someone.*

We don't like the way Mary is always fishing for a compliment.

Mary wondered if she must take the bait whenever Tom fished for a compliment.

For good: *forever, permanently.*

He intends to remain married to her for good.

I want to be with you for good.

Fair and square: *very fair.*

He won the election fair and square.

I won the game fair and square.

Fool around: *to behave in a silly way for fun.*

Don't fool around with matches.

You shouldn't fool around with dangerous chemicals.

First things first: *let's focus on dealing with the most important things before other things.*

I'm starving, so first things first, let's have something to eat.

First things first, let's see that movie.

To foot the bill: *to pay the bill; to pay for something.*

You paid for lunch last week. Let me foot the bill for dinner tonight.

She ordered drinks and then left him to foot the bill!

Face the facts: *accept that something is true (usually negative).*

I think he needs to face the facts.

Let's face the facts!

It's time for her to face the facts and move on.

Family man: *a man that likes to spend time at home with his family.*

Tom is described as being a family man.

He is a good leader and a good family man both.

Fly the coop/nest: *a child moves away from his parents' home and lives elsewhere.*

Mary flew the nest when she turned 19 years old.

Tom flew the coop when he got a full-time job in the city.

Find your feet: *to become familiar and confident with a new place, situation, etc.*

It took a while to find his feet when he started a new job.

Lucy is still new in her job; give her some time to find her feet.

Fly off the handle: *to lose one's temper suddenly; become extremely angry unexpectedly.*

You shouldn't fly off the handle about such little thing.

The teacher flies off the handle every time Tom is late.

Freak out: *to become very angry or lose control of yourself because of somebody or something.*

I freaked out when I saw her with another man.

Snakes really freaked me out.

To face the music: *be confronted with the unpleasant consequences of something you have done wrong.*

After drinking alcohol all night, the next morning he had to face the music.

He's been caught cheating. He must face the music.

Fresh as a daisy: *someone who is full of energy, completely fresh and attractive.*

Her smile is as fresh as a daisy.

His girlfriend looks as fresh as a daisy!

Full of beans: *a person who is lively, and full of energy.*

He's always full of beans in the morning.

My son is usually full of beans at the bedtime.

Feel up to: *to feel like doing or being able to do something.*

I don't feel up to working today.

After the accident, he didn't feel up to driving.

For a song: *if you buy something for a song, you buy it at a very cheap price.*

He bought the car for a song at an auction.

I bought the painting for a song two years ago.

For the time being: *at the present; at the moment.*

For the time being, I am studying Japanese.

For the time being, you can leave your suitcase here.

From now on: *from this moment and forever into the future.*

From now on, employees can wear casual clothes to work every Thursday.

From now on, I promise to be on time.

LETTER G

Give someone a hand: *to give someone help or assistance.*

Could you give me a hand with these bags? I can't make it to the sixth floor on my own!

I gave him a hand packing up his clothes and stuff.

Hey buddy, could you give me a hand? I want to move this desk.

Get the picture: *to understand something or a situation.*

It's all right, I get the picture. Don't say anymore.

He can't possibly get the picture.

It took me 30 seconds to get the picture.

To go off the deep end: *to unexpectedly become panic or very angry (to lose your temper).*

Tom went off the deep end when he lost his job.

When Mike found that his car door had been scratched, he really went off the deep end.

The woman went off the deep end when she saw her picture in the paper.

To get a hold of yourself: *to get control of your thoughts and emotions.*

She gets a hold of herself and thinks about meeting her father.

Tom gets a hold of himself and goes back into the bedroom with a smile.

To give someone a fair shake: *to give someone a fair chance.*

I hate him. He never gives me a fair shake.

I think you should give her a fair shake.

I believe that the judge will give this man a fair shake at his trial.

To go easy on someone: *to be lenient with someone (to treat someone in a gentle way).*

Go easy on him simply because he didn't know the rules.

I know she made a mistake, but go easy on her.

To get a kick out of: *to enjoy.*

He really gets a real kick out of owning his own car.

I really love books. I get a kick out of reading.

To go under the knife: *to undergo surgery (a medical operation).*

Her father is going to go under the knife because he has a bad heart.

Lucy went under the knife for her nose yesterday.

To get on someone's nerves: *to annoy someone.*

His loud voice is really getting on my nerves.

That car alarm is extremely getting on my nerves.

The dog does not stop barking which is really getting on my nerves.

Go banana: *be wild, lose control; to become very angry.*

His mom went banana on him since he was not participating in family lunch.

Got it all planned out: *ready.*

Sounds like he's got it all planned out.

Have you got it all planned out?

Get off the ground: *start in a successful way.*

The movie is very interesting, it's highly likely to get off the ground.

Don't worry, our project will get off the ground.

(to) go into: *to enter a particular type of job.*

My brother wants to go into teaching.

Her son's planning to go into journalism.

He's decided to go into law.

Go ahead: *to start or continue to do something without hesitation.*

Go ahead and eat before the food gets no longer hot.

Go ahead and make yourselves at home.

Go ahead and tell her that I'm coming.

(to) give someone a ring: *to call someone on the telephone.*

He gave her a ring for her birthday.

She gave me a ring at midnight.

Give the green light: *to grant permission.*

My parents gave me the green light to go on the camping trip.

I never give my children the green light to gambling.

Go back to the drawing board: *to start again on a new plan.*

We have to go back to the drawing board on this project.

His boss forced him to go back to the drawing board on the marketing campaign.

Get tied up: *to become very busy with something; get stuck in.*

She got tied up at work.

Sorry, I'm late. I got tied up in traffic.

Get hitched/tie the knot: *to get married.*

Bill and Sarah will get hitched next month.

After 3 years of dating each other, Tom and Mary have finally decided to tie the knot next July.

Go down in flames: *to fail completely.*

Many students went down in flames in the final exam.

After the scandal with the nanny, his career went down in flames.

Go the extra mile: *doing more than what is expected in order to achieve something.*

Mr. Mike went the extra mile to resolve my problem.

He went the extra mile, taking me to the post office.

Golden opportunity: *a very good opportunity or a chance to do something.*

He missed a golden opportunity to join the military academy.

That was a golden opportunity to invest and export into new markets.

Green with envy: *to be jealous/ to be envious (to feel very unhappy because you don't have something that someone else has)*

Tom was green with envy when he saw that I got a new car for my birthday.

My expensive house makes him green with envy.

Get cold feet: *become very nervous and afraid to do something that you had planned to do.*

She gets cold feet before marriage.

He always gets cold feet when he delivers a speech in front of a lot of people.

He got cold feet before his wedding.

Get in touch with somebody: *to contact somebody by talking or writing.*

He plans to get in touch with his friends when he returns home.

I'll get in touch with tom by telephone tomorrow.

Get mixed up: *become confused about something.*

He got mixed up with the dates and went on the wrong day.

Get rid of something: *to throw away something.*

I decided to get rid of this old furniture.

We need to get rid of that ugly old couch as rapidly as possible.

LETTER H

Hit the nail on the head: *to say something that is precisely correct or completely true.*

At last, he's hit the nail on the head!

She hit the nail on the head when she used idioms in the IELTS speaking test.

To have a mad crush on someone: *to have a great romantic interest in someone.*

Tom used to have a little crush on Lucy.

He had a crush on her when they were in high school.

To have a weakness for something: *to have a passion for something.*

My son has a weakness for chocolate.

He has a weakness for young beautiful girls.

The little girl has a weakness for cookies.

My little brother has a weakness for ice creams.

Hit the books: *to study very hard.*

I have to go home and hit the books because I have a big test tomorrow.

It's time to hit the books.

Happy camper: *someone who is really happy about something.*

Lucy was a happy camper when she was allowed to leave work early.

Peter was a happy camper when he passed the driving test.

(to) have a good time: *to enjoy yourself.*

We had a good time during the trip last week.

We had a good time together at the party yesterday.

(to have) mixed feelings: *to feel both positive and negative about someone or something.*

Sarah had mixed feelings about meeting her ex-boyfriend again.

Tom had mixed feelings about getting married to someone.

My friend had mixed feelings about giving up his job.

To have a sweet tooth: *to enjoy eating sweet food.*

I have a sweet tooth, so I will definitely have dessert!

Mary eats candy all the time. She must have a sweet tooth.

Head over heels in love: *madly in love (love someone very much).*

She's fallen head over heels in love with her boss.

Tom soon found himself head over heels in love with Mary.

Has a heart of gold: *friendly, sincere, generous.*

My aunt is a woman with a heart of gold.

Peter is so nice. He must have a heart of gold.

Head the team: *in charge of, lead a group.*

She's going to head the team in accounting.

He is going to head the team in the new advertising campaign.

Have an eye for (something): *the ability to do something well.*

She has an eye for color.

He has an eye for antique furniture.

Mary has an eye for art.

Have/get/feel butterflies in my stomach: to feel very nervous or anxious about something.

He always gets butterflies in his stomach before a test.

Mary always gets butterflies in her stomach before her big speech.

Have the hots for: *to like someone; to be attracted (sexually or romantically) to (someone).*

I think Tom has the hots for Mary.

She has the hots for him but she can't tell him. She's so shy.

Have a crush on someone: *to have a strong affection for someone.*

Sarah has a crush on Peter and she would like him to notice her.

Tom has a crush on his English teacher at school. She is so cute and great.

Hit the hay = hit the sack: *to go to bed.*

I'm pretty tired. I think it's time for me to hit the hay.

I'm going to hit the sack early since I've got to get up early tomorrow.

Hard nut to crack: *a person or thing that is difficult to understand, or deal with.*

Tom sure is a hard nut to crack. I can't figure him out.

This problem is getting me down. It's a hard nut to crack.

LETTER I

In deep water: *to be in trouble or in a difficult or dangerous situation.*

Having lost his passport, tom is now in deep water.

You'll be in deep water unless you pass that exam.

In the black: *making a profit (earn more money than you spent).*

He has worked very hard to move his account in the black.

I've managed to stay in the black for over six months.

In the red: *to owe money to the bank.*

His bank account is in the red again.

My bank account is $500 in the red.

In a pickle: *in a difficult or unpleasant situation.*

Because Tom has so much credit card debt, he's really in a pickle.

Perhaps, he'll get himself in a pickle.

In no time: *instantly.*

I'll be home in no time.

I'll be leaving home for work in no time.

He'll be back in no time.

In a bit: *in a short moment.*

Pause the movie, I'll be back in a bit.

I'll see you in a bit.

In a flash: *very quickly, in no time.*

The boat sank in a flash.

I'll be back in a flash.

He told me that he'll be here in a flash.

In deep shit: *in big trouble.*

We are in deep shit.

The thieves were in deep shit when they were caught breaking into a house.

(to be) in a bad mood: *to feel unhappy, depressed, annoyed or angry.*

Mom is in a bad mood. Stay away from her.

They were in a bad mood when they lost the game.

After his girlfriend broke up with him, Peter was in a bad mood for two weeks.

(to be) in good spirits: *to feel happy and cheerful (in a good mood).*

I hope you're in good spirits.

We are in good spirits after winning the competition today.

(to be) in charge of: *to have responsibility for (something).*

I believe that Tom can be in charge of this project.

He's in charge of the marketing department.

In a flash: *very quickly; immediately.*

The boat sank in a flash.

The accident happened in a flash.

In a heartbeat: *instantly; immediately.*

If I had the chance to study abroad, I'd go in a heartbeat.

Mary accepted the new job as a receptionist in a heartbeat.

In seventh heaven: *to be very happy.*

Tom is in seventh heaven since he's just been promoted.

Peter and Lucy have been in seventh heaven because they've just got married.

In the nick of time: *just before it's too late/ at the last possible moment.*

We got to the airport just in the nick of time.

I arrived at the train station in the nick of time.

She finished her English essay just in the nick of time.

It's raining cats and dogs: *it's raining a lot/ it is raining heavily.*

It's windy and is raining cats and dogs.

It was raining cats and dogs, so all flights were delayed.

It's as easy as pie = it's a piece of cake: *to be very easy, (not complicated).*

I don't think it's as easy as pie to get band 8.5 in the IELTS speaking test.

It's a piece of cake to drive this car.

LETTER J

Jump for joy: *be really happy/excited about something.*

He jumped for joy when he heard the news.

Mary jumped for joy when I told her the news.

Jump the gun: *start (doing) something too early.*

Tom jumped the gun when he told his friends about the surprise party next week.

Tom jumped the gun and didn't give Mary a chance to explain that it wasn't her.

LETTER K

Keep one's chin up: *to be brave and cheerful even though you are in a difficult situation.*

When you get bad news, you try to keep your chin up.

Be positive and keep your chin up. Don't quit, my friend.

To keep someone posted: *to keep someone informed.*

Keep me posted on what happened.

I'll keep you posted about my new job.

Keep in mind: *remember that.*

Keep in mind to turn off the TV before you go to bed.

Keep in mind to complete your homework by today.

Know the ropes: *have the skills and experience for a particular job.*

Mary will make fewer mistakes once she gets to know the ropes.

Tom knows the ropes much better than his friend does.

Lucy didn't know the ropes because she was new.

(to) keep one's chin up: *to stay cheerful, hopeful and positive.*

Although Mary has failed several times, she still keeps her chin up.

While everyone around Tom is downhearted, he still keeps his chin up.

LETTER L

Let's face it: *talking about the fact/truth that needs to be accepted even though you might not want it to happen.*

Let's face it, it's impossible.

Let's face it. He will not be able to achieve 8.0 Ielts if he does not study hard.

Leave no stone unturned: *to do everything you can to solve a problem or achieve something.*

Tom left no stone unturned in his search to find his stolen car.

Mary left no stone unturned in her search for her daughter.

The police left no stone unturned to look for the murderer.

Lend an ear: *to listen to someone's problems in a sympathy way.*

He lent a sympathetic ear while I told him my problems.

I lent him an ear when he needed advice on a personal situation.

To lose one's cool: *to lose one's temper; to become angry.*

She completely lost her cool when the waiter dropped her food.

My friend lost his cool with the client; as a result, he got fired from his job.

She lost her cool when she discovered her son had spilled coffee on her new dress.

(to) look on the bright side: *to think about the good/positive parts of a situation.*

She tries to look on the bright side although her cat is very sick right now.

Don't let things get you down. Stay positive and look on the bright side.

(to) lend (someone) a hand: *to help someone.*

We should lend Lucy a hand when she is in trouble.

I would lend Tom a hand if I were in your place.

Mike asked me to lend him a hand.

(to) lose one's touch: *to no longer have the ability to do something skillfully.*

He has lost his touch since he had an infection years back.

Her mom used to be an outstanding doctor, but she has lost her touch due to her illness.

(to) live with it: *to accept an unpleasant thing or situation.*

Whatever happens, we'll live with it.

I'm going to live with it since I can't change the situation.

(to) let someone go: *to fire; dismiss an employee (to end someone's job).*

After being discovered that he stole some files, his boss let him go.

(to) level with someone: *to be sincere and honest with someone about something.*

Tom decided to level with his girlfriend and tell her how he felt.

She decided to level with him about the accident.

(to) lose one's head: *to lose control and become so upset quickly.*

His mom lost her head and started yelling at him.

Lucy lost her head and said some things she regrets.

She lost her head over that man.

Lose track of time: *to forgot about the time.*

He was at work and he lost track of time!

When Tom is playing video games, he nearly always loses track of time.

Like father, like son: *expressing that a man or boy behaves in the same way as his father.*

Tom decided to study law and become a lawyer - like father, like son.

Let the cat out of the bag: *to accidentally reveal a secret, usually without intending to.*

He wanted his father's present to be a secret, but his brother let the cat out of the bag.

I tried to keep the party a surprise for my parents but my wife let the cat out of the bag.

Look like a million dollars: *luxurious, gorgeous and beautiful.*

Sarah looks like a million dollars in that new dress!

His house looks like a million dollars.

Little by little: *gradually.*

His French is improving little by little.

Little by little, she'll be super-fluent in Japanese!

LETTER M

Miss the boat: *to miss a chance or opportunity to do something by not taking action quickly enough.*

You'll miss the boat if you don't apply for this job now.

If you don't want to miss the boat, you should buy your shares in the company now.

To moonlight: *to work a second job.*

I think I have to moonlight to earn enough to feed my family.

He has to moonlight because he doesn't make enough money for rent.

(to) make up one's mind: *to make a decision.*

He can't make up his mind at all.

There are many business courses. I couldn't make up my mind which course to follow.

Tom made up his mind to marry Lucy.

Mary has made up her mind to study harder.

Make ends meet: *to earn enough money to buy the things you need without getting into debt.*

Elderly people can make ends meet on their pensions.

Many students have a difficult time trying to make ends meet.

(to) make a bundle: *to make a great deal of money.*

My father made a bundle on the stock market.

Mr. Johnson made a bundle in real estate and retired at age 45.

Made of money: *very rich.*

Do you think he is made of money?

My uncle has a very big house. He certainly is made of money.

(to) make a splash: *to become very popular.*

Denim really made a splash in the '70s.

Those new jeans really made a splash. A vast majority of young people are wearing them.

(to) make a pig of oneself: *to eat too much.*

Tom made a pig of himself at dinner.

Mary made a pig of herself at the buffet table last night.

(to) make time for: *to arrange your schedule for doing something or being with someone.*

My father is a busy doctor, but he always makes time for us.

You need to make time for regular exercise.

(to) make a fortune: *to make a lot of money.*

Her father has made a fortune through hard work.

The young man made a fortune in the stock market.

Make someone blue = bump someone out: *to make someone sad or sick.*

It made him blue to have to stay home with his wife all day.

He made his girlfriend blue yesterday.

Mean business: *to be very, very serious.*

I thought he was joking at first, but then I saw that he really meant business.

Just looking at him, I knew he meant business.

LETTER N

Needless to say = it goes without saying that: *obviously.*

Needless to say, she didn't believe him.

Needless to say, he was so excited about the journey.

It goes without saying that they are very happy about the new baby.

It goes without saying that he will be paid for the extra hours he works.

(to) not have a clue: *to know or understand nothing about something.*

Tom doesn't have a clue about what he should say to Mary.

I don't have a clue about Japanese.

I don't have a clue about how to fix a car.

(to) not sleep a wink: *to stay awake (not sleep at all).*

Peter didn't sleep a wink last night because he was worried about his exam.

We didn't sleep a wink last night due to that noise.

(to be) nuts about = to be crazy about: *to like something very much.*

She is nuts about him, but he doesn't like her.

I nuts about this new cat.

LETTER O

Once in a while: *not regularly; from time to time.*

I saw him in the bar every once in a while.

I only see her husband every once in a while at home.

Over the moon: *to be very pleased or happy about something.*

Mary was over the moon about becoming a mother.

Tom was over the moon about his new car

Lucy was over the moon about getting a new job.

On cloud nine: *extremely happy.*

Lucy was on cloud nine after finally getting a job that she liked.

They were on cloud nine after winning the competition.

Out of the blue: *without warning; unexpectedly or suddenly.*

My old high school friend called me out of the blue last night.

He arrived out of the blue while I was having dinner.

On the level: *telling the truth.*

The dealer said she's giving us the best price in town. Do you think she's on the level?

On the verge of: *very close to.*

His company is on the verge of bankruptcy.

Tom was on the verge of tears when he heard that news.

These wild animals are on the verge of extinction.

If our team win the game tomorrow, we are on the verge of winning the championship.

Out of the woods: *out of danger.*

Fortunately, we are out of the woods.

Although her father feels a little better, he's not out of the woods yet.

Out of work: *unemployed.*

He has been out of work for three months.

Thousands of people are out of work these days.

(to be) on edge: *nervous; irritable usually because you are worried about someone or something.*

He felt on edge, upset, and increasingly worried.

She felt so on edge before the interview.

One's (own) flesh and blood: *your family's members or relatives.*

You have to be nice to your siblings. They are your own flesh and blood.

The young man is my own flesh and blood.

Out of the question: *impossible.*

I'm afraid a promotion is out of the question now.

It is out of the question to digest his theory.

(to be) out of practice: *no longer good at doing something because you have not been doing it regularly.*

If you don't play guitar regularly, you can soon get out of practice.

She is out of practice at dancing. It's likely that she won't dance well tonight.

On the mark: *correct.*

In my opinion, all the things that he said were right on the mark.

His speech was on the mark.

Once in a blue moon: *very rarely/very seldom/almost never.*

My son lives in Canada and he only comes to see us once in a blue moon.

My family used to live in Tokyo, but now we only go there once in a blue moon.

Out on the town: *to enjoy yourself by going out, particularly in the evening.*

Let's go out on the town and relax ourselves.

He has gone out on the town with his friends to celebrate his birthday.

LETTER P

Put yourself in somebody's shoes: *to imagine that you are in somebody's situation or circumstances in order to understand his/her feelings, opinion, or point of view.*

I can see why you would feel that way when I put myself in your shoes.

If you put yourself in his shoes, I'm sure you don't like her.

I really appreciate his effort when I tried to put myself in his shoes.

Put all your eggs in one basket: *put all your money into one thing.*

Never put all your eggs in one basket, for example, don't invest all your money in one company.

She put all her eggs in one basket by investing all her money in stocks.

To pull yourself together: *to get control of your emotions.*

She's finding it hard to pull herself together after the accident.

It took him a while to pull himself together.

To pull one's leg: *to be kidding.*

It wasn't very fun to pull my leg like that.

If you pull her leg like that again, she'll never speak to you again.

To pop the question: *to propose marriage (ask someone to marry you).*

Mary said yes without a further thought when Tom popped the question.

Peter popped the question after dating Lucy for two years.

Tom went down on his knees and popped the question to his girlfriend last night.

To pull through: *to get through an illness or a difficult situation.*

The doctor is sure that she will pull through.

I'm afraid that the old man won't pull through.

To pop in: *to arrive without notice.*

My neighbor popped in for a visit last night.

My mother popped in at seven o'clock to see if I was at home.

(to) put up with: *to endure someone or something without complaint.*

I can't put up with her children any longer.

This machine is very awful. I can't put up with it any longer.

He is very impolite, and I can' put up with him.

(to) pay (someone) a compliment: *to give someone a compliment (saying something nice about him/her).*

He paid his girlfriend a compliment on her new haircut.

The professor paid her a compliment about her well-written thesis.

Pain in the neck: *an annoying thing or person.*

Those little kids are a real pain in the neck.

The barking dog is such a pain in the neck.

Paint the town red: *to go out and have a great time.*

We're planning to paint the town red tonight.

We painted the town red last night for my dad's 60th birthday.

To pass with flying colours: *to achieve, or accomplish something very successfully.*

He is studying hard and he will pass Ielts with flying colours.

He passed his exams with flying colours.

She passed her job interview with flying colours.

Pretty as a picture: *very pretty / beautiful.*

Mary looked pretty as a picture in her new dress.

The young woman is as pretty as a picture.

Mary was pretty as a picture after she got her hair and makeup done.

Pig out: *to eat a large amount of food in a short amount of time.*

He totally pigged out at the party last night.

The food was free at the buffet, so he pigged out.

We pigged out on chicken and roast beef at lunchtime.

Pay through the nose: *to pay too much for something.*

I usually have to pay through the nose for parking a car if I bring it into the city.

He paid through the nose to get the car fixed.

Poke around: *look around a place, typically in search of something (you can poke around on the internet, you can poke around on the streets, etc. To look for / search for something).*

Just poke around the internet, you'll find a lot of dating websites.

He poked around in his desk to see if the wallet was there.

LETTER R

Run of the mill: *average, ordinary; commonplace; mediocre.*

As far as I am concerned, she gave a fairly run-of-the-mill speech.

That restaurant has nothing special. The service and the food are just run of the mill.

To rub someone the wrong way: *to irritate or annoy someone; to get on someone's nerves.*

The way he smiles really rubs her the wrong way.

His girlfriend rubs him the wrong way.

(to) round up: *to gather people or things together.*

A group of 5 possible suspects were rounded up for questioning.

The herd of cattle are rounded up by the Cowboys.

(to) rant and rave: *to talk loudly and complain angrily about something.*

Please stop ranting and raving and listen to me for 1 minute.

She was ranting and raving about the price of food in the restaurant.

Rat race: *an activity or job, or situation that makes people too busy to relax or enjoy themselves.*

Tom decided to get out of the rat race and move to the countryside.

Working here like a rat race.

She wants to get away from the rat race.

Raining cats and dogs: *pouring rain, raining heavily.*

It's windy and is raining cats and dogs.

During the monsoon season, it rained cats and dogs.

It's raining cats and dogs outside.

To ring a bell: *to sound familiar.*

I think I heard this song somewhere. It definitely rings a bell.

His name rings a bell but I can't remember him.

Run out of steam: *to completely lose energy, motivation, or enthusiasm.*

Peter started to run out of steam after running for 15 km.

Lucy found she had run out of steam after climbing seven flights of stairs.

I'm running out of steam after spending five hours working on this essay.

LETTER S

Sleep on it: *to think more about something before making a decision.*

I can't decide what to do now. Could I sleep on it and let you know soon today?

I decided to sleep on it and give you a call tomorrow.

Sit on the fence: *to remain neutral, to delay making a decision.*

We can't sit on the fence any longer, we need to make up our mind early.

Tom is sitting on the fence, he does not know whether to say yes or no to the offer.

Soul mate: *someone with whom you have a special relationship with because you share the same feelings, attitudes, and beliefs.*

Tom has been my soul mate for a long time.

She is my wife, my best friend, and my soul mate.

Set in your ways: *not want to change your habits*

People tend to become set in their ways when they get older.

Mary was too set in her ways to make any real changes.

My grandfather is quite traditional and set in his ways.

Spring for: *pay for something.*

Tom offered to spring for the dinner last night.

Let me spring for lunch today.

(to) set eyes on: *to see (someone or something), usually for the first time.*

He told me that he loved his girlfriend the minute he set eyes on her.

My daughter has not set eyes on her new school yet.

(to) stab someone in the back: *to betray someone who trusts you.*

She almost died when her boyfriend stabbed her in the back.

He felt depressed when his son had stabbed him in the back.

(to be) stressed out: *under severe strain; worried and nervous; very anxious.*

He has been really stressed out because of work.

She is so stressed out about her job that she can't sleep at night.

(to) shake in one's shoes: *to be afraid of something.*

When he was face-to-face with the police, he was shaking in his shoes.

The old woman was shaking in her shoes for the first time of flying.

The little boy was shaking with fear.

Social butterfly: *someone who knows a lot of people or friendly with everyone.*

My sister is a social butterfly.

He doesn't really go out partying, but he is definitely a social butterfly.

Smell something fishy: *to have a feeling of doubt or suspicion about someone or something.*

I smell something fishy about this real estate deal.

I smell something fishy. I think that woman is not good.

Sick as a dog: *very sick, extremely ill.*

After last night's meal, she was sick as a dog.

Ever since John came here, he has been sick as a dog.

(as) sly as a fox: *someone who is clever, cunning, wily, and tricky.*

Many people don't like him because he is sly as a fox.

My boss is as sly as a fox.

Sleep like a baby: *to sleep very well; to sleep deeply.*

After a long, hard day at work, I slept like a baby last night.

He was very tired, so he went to bed, and slept like a baby.

Start from scratch: *to do something again from the beginning.*

Everything is completely ruined, so we should start from scratch.

Whenever my sister bakes a cake, she starts from scratch.

To show one's true colors: *to reveal someone's real personality.*

Katherine seemed nice at first, but she showed her true colors during the party.

When he tried to use a stolen credit card, he showed his true colors.

He finally showed his true colors in court.

I always regarded her as a friend, but she showed her true colors in the current emergency.

To start from square one: *to start from the very beginning.*

I have to start the game from square one.

Let's start from square one basics.

LETTER T

The in thing: *to be very fashionable.*

It's the in-thing to do at the moment.

The new iPhone is really the in thing at the moment.

This season, bald hairstyle is the in thing.

To talk someone into something: *to convince or persuade someone to do something.*

I think I can talk him into helping you.

I could probably talk her into driving you to school tomorrow.

She's managed to talk her husband into buying a new car.

To take it easy: *to rest or relax.*

Take it easy, man! Don't work so hard.

After her surgery, Sarah took it easy for a week.

Tie the knot: *to get married.*

Bill and Sarah will tie the knot next month.

After 3 years of dating each other, Tom and Mary have finally decided to tie the knot next July.

(to) talk over: *to discuss.*

We are talking over the problem.

We spent hours talking over the details of our new project.

(to) tell off: *to scold/ speak angrily to someone for doing something wrong.*

She told her son off for lying to her.

Mary told her boyfriend off after he missed their date.

The cat that ate the canary: *to look very happy / very pleased.*

He was smiling like the cat that ate the canary.

You look like the cat that ate the canary.

Throw in the towel: *to quit; to give up.*

You're almost finished! Don't throw in the towel!

Never throw in the towel.

Throw a fit: *to become very angry.*

Tom's mother threw a fit when she saw a mess that he'd made in his bedroom.

John threw a fit when he heard his car was stolen.

(like) two peas in a pod: *very similar, especially in appearance.*

Peter and his brother are like two peas in a pod.

The twins are like two peas in a pod.

LETTER U

Under one's breath: *quietly; in a very quiet voice.*

I heard his swear under his breath.

The timid girl was muttering under her breath.

(to be) up in the air: *to be uncertain.*

Everything is up in the air at the moment because he didn't get the job.

Because the management has failed to finalize the budget, the future of the project is up in the air.

To be under the weather: *do not feel well; feel sick.*

Tom was feeling a bit under the weather today, so he chose to take the day off.

I'm feeling a bit under the weather. I think I've caught a cold.

LETTER W

Watch out: *be cautious; to be careful.*

Watch out! There is a snake coming.

Watch out for that woman.

Watch out! the floor's quite slippery.

(to) work like a dog: *to work very hard.*

Mary works like a dog. She deserves the promotion.

Tom works like a dog to save money to buy a new house.

(to) work one's tail off: *to work very hard.*

He's lost one hundred dollars and works his tail off.

They work their tail off every single day for their kids!

to wine and dine: *to entertain someone with food and drink, usually at a fancy restaurant.*

He has not had a chance to wine and dine with her yet.

The company wined and dined the prospective clients.

(to) wrap up: *to finish (doing) something.*

It's 6 pm. Let's wrap up this meeting so we can go home early tonight.

We'll have time to see a movie if you wrap up your homework by 9 pm.

CONCLUSION

Thank you again for downloading this book on *"Idioms For IELTS Speaking: Master 500+ Idioms In Use Explained In 10 Minutes A Day"* and reading all the way to the end. I'm extremely grateful.

If you know of anyone else who may benefit from the useful list of 500+ Idioms In Use Explained that are revealed in this book, please help me inform them of this book. I would greatly appreciate it.

Finally, if you enjoyed this book and feel that it has added value to your work and study in any way, please take a couple of minutes to share your thoughts and post a REVIEW on Amazon. Your feedback will help me to continue to write other books of IELTS topic that helps you get the best results. Furthermore, if you write a simple REVIEW with positive words for this book on Amazon, you can help hundreds or perhaps thousands of other readers who may want to improve their IELTS lexical resource band score. Like you, they worked hard for every penny they spend on books. With the information and recommendation you provide, they would be more likely to take action right away. We really look forward to reading your review.

Thanks again for your support and good luck!

If you enjoy my book, please write a POSITIVE REVIEW on Amazon.

-- Rachel Mitchell --

CHECK OUT OTHER BOOKS

Go here to check out other related books that might interest you:

Ielts Academic Vocabulary: Master 3000+ Academic Vocabularies By Topics Explained In 10 Minutes A Day.

https://www.amazon.com/dp/B07F3X3GJ8

IELTS Listening Strategies: The Ultimate Guide with Tips, Tricks and Practice on How to Get a Target Band Score of 8.0+ in 10 Minutes a Day.

https://www.amazon.com/dp/B07845S1MG

IELTS Reading Strategies: The Ultimate Guide with Tips and Tricks on How to Get a Target Band Score of 8.0+ in 10 Minutes a Day.

Ielts Writing Task 2 Samples : Over 450 High-Quality Model Essays for Your Reference to Gain a High Band Score 8.0+ In 1 Week (Box set) https://www.amazon.com/dp/B077BYQLPG

Ielts Academic Writing Task 1 Samples: Over 450 High Quality Samples for Your Reference to Gain a High Band Score 8.0+ In 1 Week (Box set) https://www.amazon.com/dp/B077CC5ZG4

Shortcut To English Collocations: Master 2000+ English Collocations In Used Explained Under 20 Minutes A Day (5 books in 1 Box set)

https://www.amazon.com/dp/B06W2P6S22

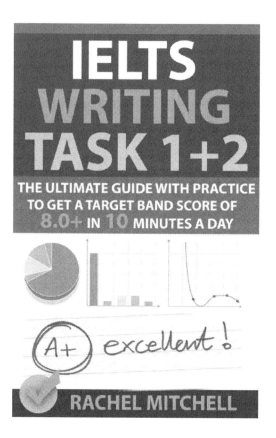

IELTS Writing Task 1 + 2: The Ultimate Guide with Practice to Get a
Target Band Score of 8.0+ In 10 Minutes a Day

https://www.amazon.com/dp/B075DFYPG6

IELTS Speaking Strategies: The Ultimate Guide With Tips, Tricks, And Practice On How To Get A Target Band Score Of 8.0+ In 10 Minutes A Day.

https://www.amazon.com/dp/B075JCW65G

Shortcut To Ielts Writing: The Ultimate Guide To Immediately
Increase Your Ielts Writing Scores.

https://www.amazon.com/dp/B01JV7EQGG

Common English Mistakes Explained With Examples: Over 600 Mistakes Almost Students Make and How to Avoid Them in Less Than 5 Minutes A Day

https://www.amazon.com/dp/B072PXVHNZ

Paraphrasing Strategies: 10 Simple Techniques For Effective
Paraphrasing In 5 Minutes Or Less

https://www.amazon.com/dp/B071DFG27Q

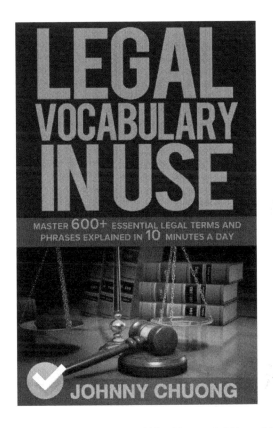

Legal Vocabulary In Use: Master 600+ Essential Legal Terms And
Phrases Explained In 10 Minutes A Day

http://www.amazon.com/dp/B01L0FKXPU

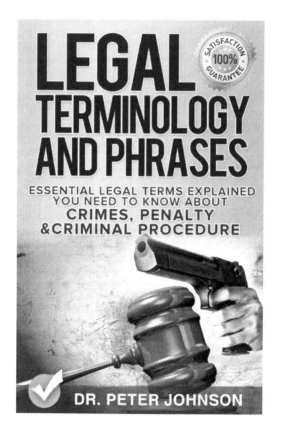

Legal Terminology And Phrases: Essential Legal Terms Explained
You Need To Know About Crimes, Penalty And Criminal Procedure

Productivity Secrets For Students: The Ultimate Guide To Improve Your Mental Concentration, Kill Procrastination, Boost Memory And Maximize Productivity In Study

http://www.amazon.com/dp/B01JS52UT6

Daughter of Strife: 7 Techniques On How To Win Back Your Stubborn Teenage Daughter

https://www.amazon.com/dp/B01HS5E3V6

Parenting Teens With Love And Logic: A Survival Guide To Overcoming The Barriers Of Adolescence About Dating, Sex And Substance Abuse

https://www.amazon.com/dp/B01JQUTNPM

http://www.amazon.com/dp/B01K0ARNA4

Made in the USA
Columbia, SC
21 June 2024